The Burning Thorn

Is poetry always worthy when it's old
And is it worthless, then, because it's new?
Reader, decide yourself if this be true:
Fools suspend judgement, waiting to be told.

Kalidasa

The Burning Thorn

an anthology of poetry selected by

GRISELDA GREAVES

MACMILLAN PUBLISHING CO., INC.

New York

First published in Great Britain 1971 by
Hamish Hamilton Children's Books Ltd.

© in this collection Griselda Greaves 1971

Macmillan Publishing Co., Inc.
866 Third Avenue, New York, N.Y. 10022
The acknowledgements on pages 187–192 constitute an
extension of this copyright page.
Library of Congress catalog card number: 70-153764
Printed in the United States of America

10   9   8   7   6   5   4   3   2

Contents

Introduction

For me, poetry is concentrated experience. To try to analyse a poem is usually to reduce it to mundane terms, because a good poem expresses what we feel but can't name. Any work of art will evoke as many different responses as there are people to witness it. There is no ultimate, correct interpretation. Also, there is no exclusiveness in the act of being a poet. A man writes because he is compelled to do so, and at times an experience will be so strong that he is forced into becoming a poet. I have therefore chosen poetry that was relevant to the anthology, whether it was by professional poets or not, and I have preferred emotional accuracy to technical skill.

I shall not try to explain what the anthology is 'about' since this would be to impose my own view. For each reader the poems will become what he makes of them.

G. G.

Ap Huw's Testament

AP HUW'S TESTAMENT

There are four verses to put down
For the four people in my life,
Father, mother, wife

And the one child. Let me begin
With her of the immaculate brow
My wife; she loves me. I know how.

My mother gave me the breast's milk
Generously, but grew mean after,
Envying me my detached laughter.

My father was a passionate man,
Wrecked after leaving the sea
In her love's shallows. He grieves in me.

What shall I say of my boy,
Tall, fair? He is young yet;
Keep his feet free of the world's net.

R. S. Thomas

FOR A CHILD EXPECTED

Lovers whose lifted hands are candles in winter,
Whose gentle ways like streams in the easy summer,
Lying together
For secret setting of a child, love what they do,
Thinking they make that candle immortal, those streams
    forever flow,
And yet do better than they know.

So the first flutter of a baby felt in the womb,
Its little signal and promise of riches to come,
Is taken in its father's name;
Its life is the body of his love, like his caress,
First delicate and strange, that daily use
Makes dearer and priceless.

Our baby was to be the living sign of our joy,
Restore to each the other's lost infancy;
To a painter's pillaging eye
Poet's coiled hearing, add the heart we might earn
By the help of love; all that our passion would yield
We put to planning our child.

The world flowed in; whatever we liked we took:
For its hair, the gold curls of the November oak
We saw on our walk;
Snowberries that make a Milky Way in the wood
For its tender hands; calm screen of the frozen flood
For our care of its childhood.

But the birth of a child is an uncontrollable glory;
Cat's cradle of hopes will hold no living baby,
Long though it lay quietly.
And when our baby stirs and struggles to be born
It compels humility: what we began
Is now its own.

For *as the sun that shines through glass
So Jesus in His Mother was.*
Therefore every human creature,
Since it shares in His nature,
In candle-gold passion or white
Sharp star should show its own way of light.
May no parental dread or dream
Darken our darling's early beam:
May she grow to her right powers
Unperturbed by passion of ours.

Anne Ridler

4

THE FONT

Thirty generations have stood and listened
By this flowering stone,
Wondering, pondering, as their child was christened;
Would he atone
For all disasters?—their son,
Now cleansed of sin,
Attain the ambitions they never won,
Would never win?

Child after child, generation on generation
Fails and fails.
Always, it seems, the subtle degradation
Of the world prevails.
Faith drowns: soon perish
The dreams they want;
Till they stand with the hopes their fathers cherish
Beside this font.

Some in stealth, raising the cover,
Have stolen water
To turn the thoughts of apprentice lover
Or merchant's daughter.
But in the end, servant or master,
In silk or cotton,
They have lain under marble and alabaster,
Or in graves forgotten. . . .

Yet we see only the outward scheme.
Within the heart
There runs a parallel but opposing stream,
Ours yet apart,
Which flows from eternity and joins it there.
Who, on that level,
Can guess the final triumph or despair
Of God and Devil?

Who can divine through what
Red Seas they crossed,
Or on what ultimate rainbowed Ararat
Each Ark was tossed?
Stand here in faith who need
Such faith. Be reconciled.
Believe that your human love may lead
The inner child.

Clive Sansom

ON THE BIRTH OF HIS SON

Families, when a child is born
Want it to be intelligent.
I, through intelligence,
Having wrecked my whole life,
Only hope the baby will prove
Ignorant and stupid.
Then he will crown a tranquil life
By becoming a Cabinet Minister.

Su Tung-P'o

A CHILD HALF-ASLEEP

Stealthily parting the small-hours silence,
a hardly-embodied figment of his brain
comes down to sit with me
as I work late.
Flat-footed, as though his legs and feet
were still asleep.

On a stool,
staring into the fire,
his dummy dangling.

Fire ignites the small coals of his eyes;
it stares back through the holes
into his head, into the darkness.

I ask what woke him?

'A wolf dreamed me.' he says.

Tony Connor

IT IS IMPOSSIBLE

It is impossible
for anyone to enter
our small world.
The adults don't
understand us
they think
we're childish.
No one can get in
our world.
It has a wall twenty feet high
and adults
have only ten feet ladders.

Ross Falconer

MAGGIE AND MILLY AND MOLLY AND MAY

maggie and milly and molly and may
went down to the beach (to play one day)

and maggie discovered a shell that sang
so sweetly she couldn't remember her troubles, and

milly befriended a stranded star
whose rays five languid fingers were;

and molly was chased by a horrible thing
which raced sideways while blowing bubbles: and

may came home with a smooth round stone
as small as a world and as large as alone.

For whatever we lose (like a you or a me)
it's always ourselves we find in the sea.

e e cummings

DIGGING FOR CHINA

'Far enough down is China,' somebody said.
'Dig deep enough and you might see the sky
As clear as at the bottom of a well.
Except it would be real—a different sky.
Then you could burrow down until you came
To China! Oh, it's nothing like New Jersey.
There's people, trees, and houses, and all that,
But much, much different. Nothing looks the same.'

I went and got the trowel out of the shed
And sweated like a coolie all that morning,
Digging a hole beside the lilac-bush,
Down on my hands and knees. It was a sort
Of praying, I suspect. I watched my hand
Dig deep and darker, and I tried and tried
To dream a place where nothing was the same.
The trowel never did break through to blue.

Before the dream could weary of itself
My eyes were tired of looking into darkness,
My sunbaked head of hanging down a hole.
I stood up in a place I had forgotten,
Blinking and staggering while the earth went round
And showed me silver barns, the fields dozing
In palls of brightness, patens growing and gone
In the tides of leaves, and the whole sky china blue.
Until I got my balance back again
All that I saw was China, China, China.

Richard Wilbur

11

CHILD ON TOP OF A GREENHOUSE

The wind billowing out the seat of my britches,
My feet crackling splinters of glass and dried putty,
The half-grown chrysanthemums staring up like accusers,
Up through the streaked glass, flashing with sunlight,
A few white clouds all rushing eastward,
A line of elms plunging and tossing like horses,
And everyone, everyone pointing up and shouting!

Theodore Roethke

AUTOBIOGRAPHY

In my childhood trees were green
And there was plenty to be seen.

Come back early or never come.

My father made the walls resound,
He wore his collar the wrong way round.

Come back early or never come.

My mother wore a yellow dress;
Gently, gently, gentleness.

Come back early or never come.

When I was five the black dreams came;
Nothing after was quite the same.

Come back early or never come.

The dark was talking to the dead;
The lamp was dark beside my bed.

Come back early or never come.

When I woke they did not care;
Nobody, nobody was there.

Come back early or never come.

When my silent terror cried,
Nobody, nobody replied.

Come back early or never come.

I got up; the chilly sun
Saw me walk away alone.

Come back early or never come.

                    Louis MacNeice

THE LIME-TREE

The lime-tree fruited in our poultry yard;
Sometimes I dream and see it; still quite small,
I stand in nightclothes, barefoot; on the ground
My shadow stretches, shaped like a hunched bird
And cast by moonlight; then I'm tiptoe tall
To take one of the limes into my hand.

It's best the dream ends there: that now the fowls
Their draggled plumage turned to silvery mail,
Don't rouse to mock me as I slip on dung
While tugging at the fruit—I fall, it rolls
Out of my reach; the hens more coarsely rail—
I try to shout them down, can't find my tongue.

Salt on my lips I taste my silent tears;
The deep sobs rack me, choke me till I wake
To find the hand still clenched that held the cheat;
All day that hand will show four sickle scars
Upon the palm, and, as I wait daybreak,
Perfume of lime clings like the sweaty sheet.

Edward Lucie-Smith

KOKO OLORO
From a children's propitiation chant

Dolorous kno
Plead for me
Farm or hill
Plead for me
Stream and wind
Take my voice
Home or road
Plead for me
On this shoot, I
Bind your leaves
Stalk and bud
Berries three
On the threshold
Cast my voice
Knot of bitters
Plead for me.

Wole Soyinka

THE IRISH DANCER

Ich am of Irlaunde,
Ant of the holy londe
   Of Irlande.
Gode sire, pray ich the,
For of saynte charité,
Come ant daunce wyth me
   In Irlaunde.

Anon

'OUT, OUT—'

The buzz saw snarled and rattled in the yard
And made dust and dropped stove-length sticks of wood,
Sweet-scented stuff when the breeze drew across it.
And from there those that lifted eyes could count
Five mountain ranges one behind the other
Under the sunset far into Vermont.
And the saw snarled and rattled, snarled and rattled,
As it ran light, or had to bear a load.
And nothing happened: day was all but done.
Call it a day, I wish they might have said
To please the boy by giving him the half hour
That a boy counts so much when saved from work.
His sister stood beside them in her apron
To tell them 'Supper'. At the word, the saw,
As if to prove saws knew what supper meant,
Leaped out at the boy's hand, or seemed to leap—
He must have given the hand. However it was,
Neither refused the meeting. But the hand!
The boy's first outcry was a rueful laugh,
As he swung toward them holding up the hand
Half in appeal, but half as if to keep
The life from spilling. Then the boy saw all—
Since he was old enough to know, big boy
Doing a man's work, though a child at heart—
He saw all spoiled. 'Don't let him cut my hand off—
The doctor, when he comes. Don't let him, sister!'
So. But the hand was gone already.

The doctor put him in the dark of ether.
He lay and puffed his lips out with his breath.
And then—the watcher at his pulse took fright.
No one believed. They listened at his heart.
Little—less—nothing!—and that ended it.
No more to build on there. And they, since they
Were not the one dead, turned to their affairs.

Robert Frost

THE LESSON

'Your father's gone,' my bald headmaster said.
His shiny dome and brown tobacco jar
Splintered at once in tears. It wasn't grief.
I cried for knowledge which was bitterer
Than any grief. For there and then I knew
That grief has uses—that a father dead
Could bind the bully's fist a week or two;
And then I cried for shame, then for relief.

I was a month past ten when I learnt this:
I still remember how the noise was stilled
In school-assembly when my grief came in.
Some goldfish in a bowl quietly sculled
Around their shining prison on its shelf.
They were indifferent. All the other eyes
Were turned towards me. Somewhere in myself
Pride, like a goldfish, flashed a sudden fin.

                                        Edward Lucie-Smith

MOTHER AND SON

At nine o'clock in the morning
My son said to me:
Mother, he said, from the wet streets
The clouds are removed and the sun walks
Without shoes on the warm pavements.
There are girls biddable at the corners
With teeth cleaner than your white plates;
The sharp clatter of your dishes
Is less pleasant to me than their laughter.
The day is building; before its bright walls
Fall in dust, let me go
Beyond the front garden without you
To find glasses unstained by tears,
To find mirrors that do not reproach
My smooth face; to hear above the town's
Din life roaring in the veins.

R. S. Thomas

WE REAL COOL

THE POOL PLAYERS.
SEVEN AT THE GOLDEN SHOVEL.

We real cool. We
Left school. We

Lurk late. We
Strike straight. We

Sing sin. We
Thin gin. We

Jazz June. We
Die soon.

Gwendolyn Brooks

BOY DRIVING HIS FATHER TO CONFESSION

Four times now I have seen you as another
Man, a grown-up friend, less than a father;
Four times found chinks in the paternal mail
To find you lost like me, quite vulnerable.
Twice it was your incredible distress,
Once your adult laughter, now your weakness.
There was the time when my child-brother died
And in the porch, among the men, you cried.
Again, last year, I was shocked at your tears
When my mother's plane took off: in twelve years
You had not been apart for one whole day
Until this long-threatened, two-week holiday.
I left you lonely at the barrier,
Was embarrassed later when you stood a beer.
The third time you made a man of me
By telling me an almost smutty story
In a restaurant toilet; we both knew
This was an unprecedented breakthrough.

Today, a sinner, and shy about it,
You asked me to drive up to church, and sit
Morose as ever, telling me to slow
On corners or at pot-holes that I know
As well as you do. What is going on
Beneath that thick grey hair? What confession
Are you preparing? Do you tell sins as I would?
Does the same hectic rage in our one blood?

Here at the churchyard I am slowing down
To meet you, the fourth time, on common ground.
You grunt and slam the door. I watch another
Who gropes as awkwardly to know his father.

Seamus Heaney

A Mound of Planets

AS I LAY WITH MY HEAD IN YOUR LAP
CAMERADO . . .

As I lay with my head in your lap camerado,
The confession I made I resume, what I said to
    you and the open air I resume,
I know I am restless and make others so,
I know my words are weapons full of danger,
    full of death,
For I confront peace, security, and all the settled
    laws, to unsettle them,
I am more resolute because all have denied me
    than I could ever have been had all accepted
    me,
I heed not and have never heeded either experience,
    cautions, majorities, nor ridicule,
And the threat of what is call'd hell is little or
    nothing to me,
And the lure of what is call'd heaven is little or
    nothing to me;
Dear camerado! I confess I have urged you
    onward with me, and still urge you, without
    the least idea what is our destination,
Or whether we shall be victorious, or utterly
    quell'd and defeated.

Walt Whitman

I WOULD LIKE TO DESCRIBE

I would like to describe the simplest emotion
joy or sadness
but not as others do
reaching for shafts of rain or sun

I would like to describe a light
which is being born in me
but I know it does not resemble
any star
for it is not so bright
not so pure
and is uncertain

I would like to describe courage
without dragging behind me a dusty lion
and also anxiety
without shaking a glass full of water

to put it another way
I would give all metaphors
in return for one word
drawn out of my breast like a rib
for one word
contained within the boundaries
of my skin

but apparently this is not possible

and just to say—I love
I run around like mad
picking up handfuls of birds
and my tenderness
which after all is not made of water
asks the water for a face

and anger
different from fire
borrows from it
a loquacious tongue

so is blurred
so is blurred
in me
what white-haired gentlemen
separated once and for all
and said
this is the subject
and this is the object

we fall asleep
with one hand under our head
and with the other in a mound of planets

our feet abandon us
and taste the earth
with their tiny roots
which next morning
we tear out painfully

Zbigniew Herbert

THIS LAND

Give me a harsh land to wring music from,
brown hills, and dust, with dead grass
straw to my bricks.

Give me words that are cutting-harsh
as wattle-bird notes in dusty gums
crying at noon.

Give me a harsh land, a land that
swings, like heart and blood,
from heat to mist.

Give me a land that like my heart
scorches its flowers of spring,
then floods upon its summer ardour.

Give me a land where rain
is rain that would beat high heads low.
Where wind howls at the windows

and patters dust on tin roofs
while it hides the summer sun
in a mud-red shirt.

Give my words sun and rain,
desert and heat and mist,
spring flowers, and dead grass,
blue sea and dusty sky,

song-birds and harsh cries,
strength and austerity
that this land has.

Ian Mudie

TOTEM

I must hide him in my innermost veins
The Ancestor whose stormy hide is shot with lightning and
    thunder
My animal protector, I must hide him
That I may not break the barriers of scandal:
He is my faithful blood that demands fidelity
Protecting my naked pride against
Myself and the scorn of luckier races.

Léopold Sédar Senghor

MR BLEANEY

'This was Mr Bleaney's room. He stayed
The whole time he was at the Bodies, till
They moved him.' Flowered curtains, thin and
    frayed,
Fall to within five inches of the sill,

Whose window shows a strip of building land,
Tussocky, littered. 'Mr Bleaney took
My bit of garden properly in hand.'
Bed, upright chair, sixty-watt bulb, no hook

Behind the door, no room for books or bags—
'I'll take it.' So it happens that I lie
Where Mr Bleaney lay, and stub my fags
On the same saucer-souvenir, and try

Stuffing my ears with cotton-wool, to drown
The jabbering set he egged her on to buy.
I know his habits—what time he came down,
His preference for sauce to gravy, why

He kept on plugging at the four aways—
Likewise their yearly frame: the Frinton folk
Who put him up for summer holidays,
And Christmas at his sister's house in Stoke.

But if he stood and watched the frigid wind
Tousling the clouds, lay on the fusty bed
Telling himself that this was home, and grinned,
And shivered, without shaking off the dread

That how we live measures our own nature,
And at his age having no more to show
Than one hired box should make him pretty sure
He warranted no better, I don't know.

Philip Larkin

HAWTHORN WHITE

Hawthorn white, hawthorn red
Hanging in the garden at my head
Tell me simple, tell me true
When comes the winter what must I do?

I have a house with chimneys four
I have a silver bell on the door,
A single hearth and a single bed.
   Not enough, the hawthorn said.

I have a lute, I have a lyre
I have a yellow cat by my fire,
A nightingale to my tree is tied.
   That bird looks sick, the hawthorn sighed.

I write on paper pure as milk
I lie on sheets of Shantung silk,
On my green breast no sin has snowed.
   You'll catch your death, the hawthorn crowed.

My purse is packed with a five-pound note
The watchdogs in my garden gloat.
I blow the bagpipe down my side.
   Better blow your safe, the hawthorn cried.

My pulse is steady as my clock
My wits are wise as the weathercock.
Twice a year we are overhauled.
   It's Double Summer-Time! the hawthorn called.

I have a horse with wings for feet
I have chicken each day to eat.
When I was born the church-bells rang.
   Only one at a time, the hawthorn sang.

I have a cellar, I have a spread
The bronze blood runs round my bulkhead.
Why is my heart as light as lead?
   Love is not there, the hawthorn said.

                        Charles Causley

SECOND NIGHT IN N.Y.C. AFTER 3 YEARS

I was happy I was bubbly drunk
The street was dark
I waved to a young policeman
He smiled
I went up to him and like a flood of gold
Told him all about my prison youth
About how noble and great some convicts were
And about how I just returned from Europe
Which wasn't half as enlightening as prison
And he listened attentively I told no lie
Everything was truth and humor
He laughed
He laughed
And it made me so happy I said:
'Absolve it all, kiss me!'
'No no no no!' he said
  and hurried away.

Gregory Corso

THE BAD THING

Sometimes just being alone seems the bad thing.
Solitude can swell until it blocks the sun.
It hurts so much, even fear, even worrying
Over past and future, get stifled. It has won,
You think; this is the bad thing, it is here.
Then sense comes; you go to sleep, or have
Some food, write a letter or work, get something
    clear.
Solitude shrinks; you are not all its slave.

Then you think: the bad thing inhabits yourself.
Just being alone is nothing; not pain, not balm.
Escape, into poem, into pub, wanting a friend
Is not avoiding the bad thing. The high shelf
Where you stacked the bad thing, hoping for calm,
Broke. It rolled down. It follows you to the end.

John Wain

LET'S ALL MEET AND HAVE
A PARTY SOMETIME

The way I walked that Sunday night, I was one
    of them;
one of the slow old walkers who kept passing me,
one of the people I saw between brick houses and
    on stone pavements,
one of those with no-one to pass away streams of
    days with,
dreams of conversation, as shallow, as satisfying
as the life-rills of asphalt gutters;
one of those with the baggy trousers of a suit,
the coat, the hat, all the clothes of age,
of defeat, of tiredness, of dull pain;
of loneliness.
And I, like them, hope to escape.

John Birkby

NOT WAVING BUT DROWNING

Nobody heard him, the dead man,
But still he lay moaning:
I was much further out than you thought
And not waving but drowning.

Poor chap, he always loved larking
And now he's dead
It must have been too cold for him his heart gave way,
They said.

Oh no no no, it was too cold always
(Still the dead one lay moaning)
I was much too far out all my life
And not waving but drowning.

Stevie Smith

THE WEDDING

Because there was no moon
our young sister was married
by the light of the stars.
She walked slowly the length
of the aisle of the river,
the stones arched above her
and the windows were water
patterned with lilies and garlands
    of reeds.
She walked with her bridegroom
down the nave of the sea
to the peal of the waves
and lightly-flung sand grains.
We called to her, called to her
and the echo returned to us
from the vaults of the ocean.
Because there was no moon
our young sister was married
by the light of the stars
and her heart was closed
within a light ring of coral.

Roland Gant

THESE DREAMINGS MINE

give me time i cannot think   for
                              outside my window the sky
                                is drifting away
and the noise
                              of the flowers
        so sweet so sad so fresh
                                        after so many days
i have closed my window
        now that i cannot grasp
                                        quite
                                          what to say
about you
                        so pale the flowers so graceful
        the lilies growing from your skin
                                        i thought
        i could pick
                                        till i found
        they had roots
                              and then
and then
                        of course i couldnt do it
                                in the fields
        the grass is cool and fresh
                                the air is the breath
        off the stars
                              far away
                                but the fields

42

                     are far off
                                    over the horizon outside
                                          my window
          n i think
                               who gives a shit anyway
i say   i say
          nothing   but i do i do
          has changed its   gently
          all the   gently
               same   the sun plays
          to me   on the water
whats the difference   lilies stirring
          lilies all   ruffled in
               die   the
flowers to   swaying
     dust   breeze
                         lilies
                         falling from the sky
                            breaking so white
                               breaking

     and falling
          so quietly
                                    and gone
                                          in
     the time it takes for your breath
               so far
                         and whispering vanished
     gone
                         these dreamings mine

                                        James O. Taylor

43

LA FIGLIA CHE PIANGE

O quam te memorem virgo ...

Stand on the highest pavement of the stair—
Lean on a garden urn—
Weave, weave the sunlight in your hair—
Clasp your flowers to you with a pained surprise—
Fling them to the ground and turn
With a fugitive resentment in your eyes:
But weave, weave the sunlight in your hair.

So I would have had him leave,
So I would have had her stand and grieve,
So he would have left
As the soul leaves the body torn and bruised,
As the mind deserts the body it has used.
I should find
Some way incomparably light and deft,
Some way we both should understand,
Simple and faithless as a smile and shake of the hand.

She turned away, but with the autumn weather
Compelled my imagination many days,
Many days and many hours:
Her hair over her arms and her arms full of flowers.
And I wonder how they should have been together!
I should have lost a gesture and a pose.
Sometimes these cogitations still amaze
The troubled midnight and the noon's repose.

T. S. Eliot

44

The Hour of Knowing

FOR ANNE GREGORY

'Never shall a young man,
Thrown into despair
By those great honey-coloured
Ramparts at your ear,
Love you for yourself alone
And not your yellow hair.'

'But I can get a hair-dye
And set such colour there,
Brown, or black, or carrot,
That young men in despair
May love me for myself alone
And not my yellow hair.'

'I heard an old religious man
But yesternight declare
That he had found a text to prove
That only God, my dear,
Could love you for yourself alone
And not your yellow hair.'

W. B. Yeats

PLUCKING THE RUSHES

(A boy and a girl are sent to gather rushes for thatching)

Green rushes with red shoots,
Long leaves bending to the wind—
You and I in the same boat
Plucking rushes at the Five Lakes.
We started at dawn from the orchid-island:
We rested under the elms till noon.
You and I plucking rushes
Had not plucked a handful when night came!

Anon

WAIT . . .

Wait:
Love is so delicate,
So tenuously stemming and unfolding,
That you should be content
To know it immanent,
Who crave now for the having and the holding.
Wait:
Do not perpetrate
The common blasphemy, the clawing error,
So avid to secure
That which will not endure
Whose aftermath is the heart's hell of terror.

P. D. Cummins

DOG-TIRED

If she would come to me here
  Now the sunken swaths
  Are glittering paths
To the sun, and the swallows cut clear
Into the setting sun! if she came to me here!

If she would come to me now,
Before the last-mown harebells are dead;
While that vetch-clump still burns red!
Before all the bats have dropped from the bough
To cool in the night; if she came to me now!

The horses are untackled, the chattering machine
Is still at last. If she would come
We could gather up the dry hay from
The hill-brow, and lie quite still, till the green
Sky ceased to quiver, and lost its active sheen.

I should like to drop
On the hay, with my head on her knee,
And lie dead still, while she
Breathed quiet above me; and the crop
Of stars grew silently.

I should like to lie still
As if I was dead; but feeling
Her hand go stealing
Over my face and my head, until
This ache was shed.

D. H. Lawrence

NOT TO SLEEP

Not to sleep all the night long, for pure joy,
Counting no sheep and careless of chimes,
Welcoming the dawn confabulation
Of birds, her children, who discuss idly
Fanciful details of the promised coming—
Will she be wearing red, or russet, or blue,
Or pure white?—whatever she wears, glorious:
Not to sleep all the night long, for pure joy,
This is given to few but at last to me,
So that when I laugh and stretch and leap from bed
I shall glide downstairs, my feet brushing the carpet
In courtesy to civilized progression,
Though, did I wish, I could soar through the open window
And perch on a branch above, acceptable ally
Of the birds still alert, grumbling gently together.

Robert Graves

THE LOVER'S SHIRT

As I was washing under a span
of the bridge of Cardigan
and in my hand my lover's shirt
with a golden beetle to drub the dirt,
a man came to me on a steed,
broad in shoulder, proud in speed,
and he asked me if I'd sell
the shirt of the lad I love so well.

But I said I wouldn't sell
for a hundred pounds and packs as well,
nor if the grass of two ridges were deep
in wethers and the whitest sheep,
nor if two hay meadows were choked
with oxen which were ready yoked,
nor if St. David's nave were filled
with herbs all pressed but not distilled.
Not even for all that would I sell
the shirt of the lad I love so well.

Anon

SONG OF A COMMON LOVER

Don't love me, my sweet,
like your shadow
for shadows fade at evening
and I want to keep you
right up to cockcrow;
nor like pepper
which makes the belly hot
for then I couldn't take you
when I'm hungry;
nor like a pillow
for we'd be together in the hours of sleep
but scarcely meet by day;
nor like rice
for once swallowed you think no more of it;
nor like soft speeches
for they quickly vanish;
nor like honey,
sweet indeed but too common.
Love me like a beautiful dream,
your life in the night,
my hope in the day;
like a piece of money,
ever with me on earth,
and for the great journey
a faithful comrade;
like a calabash,
intact, for drawing water;
in pieces, bridges for my guitar.

Flavien Ranaivo

54

BECAUSE I BREATHE NOT LOVE TO EVERY ONE

Because I breathe not love to every one,
Nor doe not use sette colours for to weare,
Nor nourish speciall locks of vowèd haire,
Nor give each speech a full point of a grone,
The Courtly nymphes, acquainted with the mone
Of them which in their lips Love's standard beare:
What, he! (say they of me): now I dare sweare
He cannot love; no, no, let him alone.
And thinke so still, so Stella know my minde;
Profess in deede I do not, Cupid's art;
But you, fair maides, at length this true shall find,
That his right badge is but worne in the hart:
Dumbe swans, not chattring pies, do lovers prove;
They love indeed who quake to say they love.

Sir Philip Sidney

PARLOUR PIECE

With love so like fire they dared not
Let it out into strawy small talk;
With love so like a flood they dared not
Let out a trickle lest the whole crack,

These two sat speechlessly:
Pale cool tea in tea-cups chaperoned
Stillness, silence, the eyes
Where fire and flood strained.

Ted Hughes

SEEN THROUGH THE TREES BEHIND WHICH YOU'RE WALKING

Seen through the trees behind which you're walking
that girl, soaking and pale,
and the boy running her to shelter
near where the suburbs fade.

Let them find there a makeshift bed
where they can lie and listen
to the thin rain teeming and city droning
near to where they've hidden.

She'll be young and he not much older,
their bodies come alive,
their time there will stand against
the closing down of dreams.

And both lying, drenched, dishevelled
in a time when their world's shrunk, gone stale,
they'll sense their loving on such days
open it a while.

For in some obscene future moment
something in them will have shrivelled
choked by the ignorant mind
that gives love a local duty.

Let them lie down together
and not with another's guilt,
let them touch as the rain touches
the world and all its shapes.

For as his hands rest now wet against her
so they'll rest in time
against the memory of a shelter
where they stopped once in the rain.

Brian Patten

THE VOICE

Safe in the magic of my woods
  I lay, and watched the dying light.
Faint in the pale high solitudes,
  And washed with rain and veiled by night,

Silver and blue and green were showing.
  And the dark woods grew darker still;
And birds were hushed; and peace was growing;
  And quietness crept up the hill;

And no wind was blowing . . .

And I knew
That this was the hour of knowing,
And the night and the woods and you
Were one together, and I should find
Soon in the silence the hidden key
Of all that had hurt and puzzled me—
Why you were you, and the night was kind,
And the woods were part of the heart of me.

And there I waited breathlessly,
Alone; and slowly the holy three,
The three that I loved, together grew
One, in the hour of knowing,
Night, and the woods, and you—

And suddenly
There was an uproar in my woods,
The noise of a fool in mock distress,
Crashing and laughing and blindly going,
Of ignorant feet and a swishing dress,
And a Voice profaning the solitudes.

The spell was broken, the key denied me,
And at length your flat clear voice beside me
Mouthed cheerful clear flat platitudes.

You came and quacked beside me in the wood.
You said, 'The view from here is very good!'
You said, 'It's nice to be alone a bit!'
And, 'How the days are drawing out!' you said.
You said, 'The sunset's pretty, isn't it?'

By God! I wish—I wish that you were dead!

Rupert Brooke

SWEET, LET ME GO

Sweet, let me go! sweet, let me go!
What do you mean to vex me so?
Cease your pleading force!
Do you think thus to extort remorse?
Now, now! no more! alas, you overbear me,
And I would cry,—but some would hear, I fear me.

Anon

FARMER'S POINT OF VIEW

I own certain acre-scraps of woodland, scattered
On undulating ground; enough to lie hidden in. So,

About three times a year, and usually August,
Pairs of people come to one or another patch. They stray

Around the edges first, plainly wanting some excuse
To go on in; then talking, as if not concerned,

And always of something else, not what they intend,
They find their way, by one or another approach,

To conducting sexual liaisons—on *my* land.
I've tried to be careful. I haven't mentioned 'love'

Or any idea of passion or consummation;
And I won't call them 'lovers' because I can't say

If they come from affection, or lust, or blackmail,
Or if what they do has any particular point

For either or both (and who can say what 'love' means?)
So what am I saying? I'd like to see people pondering

What unalterable acts they might be committing
When they step down, full of plans, from their trains or cars.

I am not just recording their tragic, or comic, emotions,
Or even the subtler hazards of owning land—

I am honestly concerned. I want to say, politely,
That I worry when I think what they're about:

I want them to explain themselves before they use my woods.

Alan Brownjohn

RIP.

A girl in our village makes love in the churchyard.
She doesn't care who, but it must be the churchyard.
They say she prefers the old part to the new.
Green granite chippings, maybe,
Rankle. Worn slabs welcome.
And after, in her bedroom,
She sees the mirror's view
Of her shoulder embossed
In Loving Memory.

Ann, why do you do it, you've eight 'O' Levels?
Why not, Ann? If bones remember, you'll give them joy.
It's as good a place as any,
Close by nave, rood screen, chapel at ease,
Peal of the bells,
Bob Singles and Grandsire Doubles,
And when you half close your eyes,
The horned gargoyles choose.

But it has to happen.
Oh, Ann, tonight you were levelled.
William Jones, late of this parish,
Was cold beneath you, and his great-great-grandson
Warm above; and you rose,
Though your shoulder didn't know it,
In Glorious Expectation of the Life to Come.

Alan Garner

64

FIFTEEN BOYS

Fifteen boys and, maybe, more,
or fewer than fifteen, maybe,
said to me
in frightened voices:
'Let's go to a movie or the Museum of Fine Arts.'
I answered them more or less like this:
'I haven't time.'
Fifteen boys presented me with snowdrops.
Fifteen boys in broken voices
said to me:
'I'll never stop loving you.'
I answered them more or less like this:
'We'll see.'

Fifteen boys are now living a quiet life.
They have done their heavy chores
of snowdrops, despair and writing letters.
Girls love them—
some more beautiful than me,
others less beautiful.
Fifteen boys with a show of freedom, and at times spite
salute me when we meet,
salute in me, when we meet,
their liberation, normal sleep and regular meals.

In vain you come to me, last boy.
I shall place your snowdrops in a glass of water,

and silver bubbles will cover the stems . . .
But, you see, you too will cease to love me,
and, mastering yourself, you'll talk in a superior way,
as though you'd mastered me,
and I'll walk off down the street, down the street. . .

Bella Akhmadulina

THE LETTER

I take my pen in hand

there was a meadow
beside a field of oats, beside a wood,
beside a road, beside a day spread out
green at the edges, yellow at the heart.
The dust lifted a little, a finger's breadth;
the word of the wood pigeon travelled slow,
a slow half-pace behind the tick of time.

To tell you I am well and thinking of you

and of the walk through the meadow, and of another walk
along the neat piled ruin of the town
under a pale heaven empty of all but death
and rain beginning. The river ran beside.

It has been a long time since I wrote. I have no news.

I put my head between my hands and hope
my heart will choke me. I put out my hand
to touch you and touch air. I turn to sleep
and find a nightmare, hollowness and fear.

And by the way, I have had no letter now
For eight weeks, it must be

a long eight weeks,
because you have nothing to say, nothing at all,
not even to record your emptiness
or guess what's to become of you, without love.

67

I know that you have cares,

ashes to shovel, broken glass to mend
and many a cloth to patch before the sunset.

Write to me soon and tell me how you are.

if you still tremble, sweat and glower, still stretch
a hand for me at dusk, play me the tune,
show me the leaves and towers, the lamb, the rose.

Because I always wish to hear of you

and feel my heart swell and the blood run out
at the ungraceful syllable of your name
said through the scent of stocks, the little snore of fire,
the shoreless waves of symphony, the murmuring night.

I will end this letter now. I am yours with love.

Always with love, with love.

Elizabeth Riddell

SONG

Goe, and catche a falling starre,
  Get with child a mandrake roote,
Tell me, where all past yeares are,
  Or who cleft the Divels foot,
Teach me to heare Mermaides singing,
  Or keep off envies stinging,
        And finde
        What winde
Serves to advance an honest minde.

If thou beest borne to strange sights,
  Things invisible to see,
Ride ten thousand daies and nights,
  Till age snow white haires on thee,
Thou, when thou retorn'st, wilt tell mee
All strange wonders that befell thee,
        And sweare
        No where
Lives a woman true, and faire.

If thou findst one, let mee know,
  Such a Pilgrimage were sweet;
Yet doe not, I would not goe,
  Though at next doore wee might meet,
Though shee were true, when you met her,
And last, till you write your letter,
        Yet shee
        Will bee
False, ere I come, to two, or three.

                          John Donne

JUDAS

I gave my heart to a tin pan bitch
Handed it her on a silver platter
Take it or leave it I softly said
(Holding my breath in the midnight hours
And the tall tree hid her golden head)

I can be bitter she smiling said
I kissed her lips and her empty head
And smiled inside at her silly prattle
I called it love and I laughed instead
She took my love and cut me dead

I paid my money to my flat-eyed father
I took the gun and the thirty bullets
And blew out her brains on the Sabbath day
(Remember that day and keep it holy)
I shall love my love till my dying day

I caught her ghost as it came riding
Her hair behind like a flying mane
And I rode my love to the crack of doom
I followed her down to the final darkness
To hang myself as the cock crowed noon

70

And what was the use? My father jeered
Now are you happy you're finally dead?
What of your love and her golden head?
I shall love my love till my dying day
Though she take my love and leave me dead

But damned be my father I shall softly pray
Who stole my love and my life away.

Andrew Baster

SONNET

I said I splendidly loved you; it's not true.
　　Such long swift tides stir not a land-locked sea.
On gods or fools the high risk falls—on you—
　　The clean clear bitter-sweet that's not for me.
Love soars from earth to ecstasies unwist.
　　Love is flung Lucifer-like from Heaven to Hell.
But—there are wanderers in the middle mist,
　　Who cry for shadows, clutch, and cannot tell
Whether they love at all, or, loving, whom:
　　An old song's lady, a fool in fancy dress,
Or phantoms, or their own face on the gloom;
　　For love of Love, or from heart's loneliness.
Pleasure's not theirs, nor pain. They doubt, and sigh,
And do not love at all. Of these am I.

Rupert Brooke

ADRIAN HENRI'S TALKING AFTER CHRISTMAS BLUES

Well I woke up this mornin' it was Christmas Day
And the birds were singing the night away
I saw my stocking lying on the chair
Looked right to the bottom but you weren't there
there was
        apples
          oranges
            chocolates
              . . . . aftershave
—but no you.

So I went downstairs and the dinner was fine
There was pudding and turkey and lots of wine
And I pulled those crackers with a laughing face
Till I saw there was no one in your place
there was
        mincepies
          brandy
            nuts and raisins
              . . . . mashed potato
—but no you.

Now it's New Year and it's Auld Lang Syne
And it's 12 o'clock and I'm feeling fine
Should Auld Acquaintance be Forgot?

I don't know girl, but it hurts a lot
there was
        whisky
          vodka
            dry Martini (stirred
              but not shaken)
. . . . and 12 New Year resolutions
—all of them about you.

So it's all the best for the year ahead
As I stagger upstairs and into bed
Then I looked at the pillow by my side
. . . . I tell you baby I almost cried
there'll be
        Autumn
        Summer
         Spring
           . . . . and Winter
—all of them without you.

Adrian Henri

WHY SO PALE AND WAN?

Why so pale and wan, fond lover?
  Prithee, why so pale?
Will, when looking well can't move her,
  Looking ill prevail?
  Prithee, why so pale?

Why so dull and mute, young sinner?
  Prithee, why so mute?
Will, when speaking well can't win her,
  Saying nothing do't?
  Prithee, why so mute?

Quit, quit for shame; this will not move,
  This cannot take her;
If of herself she will not love,
  Nothing can make her.
  The devil take her.

Sir John Suckling

COME AWAY, MY LOVE

Come away, my love, from streets
Where unkind eyes divide,
And shop windows reflect our difference.
In the shelter of my faithful room rest.

There, safe from opinions, being behind
Myself, I can see only you;
And in my dark eyes your grey
Will dissolve.
            The candlelight throws
Two dark shadows on the wall
Which merge into one as I close beside you.

When at last the lights are out,
And I feel your hand in mine,
Two human breaths join in one,
And the piano weaves
Its unchallenged harmony.

Joseph Kariuki

THE STARRED COVERLET

A difficult achievement for true lovers
Is to lie mute, without embrace or kiss,
Without a rustle or a smothered sigh,
Basking each in the other's glory.

Let us not undervalue lips or arms
As reassurances of constancy,
Or speech as necessary communication
When troubled hearts go groping through the dusk;

Yet lovers who have learned this last refinement—
To lie apart, yet sleep and dream together
Motionless under their starred coverlet—
Crown love with wreaths of myrtle.

Robert Graves

YOUR NAME UPON THE SAND

Well I remember how you smiled
  To see me write your name upon
The soft sea-sand . . . 'O! What a child!
  You think you're writing upon stone!'
I have since written what no tide
  Shall ever wash away, what men
Unborn shall read o'er ocean wide
  And find Ianthe's name agen.

Walter Savage Landor

As Mirrors Live

LES SYLPHIDES

Life in a day: he took his girl to the ballet;
Being shortsighted himself could hardly see it—
    The white skirts in the grey
    Glade and the swell of the music
    Lifting the white sails.

Calyx upon calyx, canterbury bells in the breeze
The flowers on the left mirror to the flowers on the right
    And the naked arms above
    The powdered faces moving
    Like seaweed in a pool.

Now, he thought, we are floating—ageless, oarless—
Now there is no separation, from now on
    You will be wearing white
    Satin and a red sash
    Under the waltzing trees.

But the music stopped, the dancers took their curtain,
The river had come to a lock—a shuffle of programmes—
    And we cannot continue down
    Stream unless we are ready
    To enter the lock and drop.

So they were married—to be the more together—
And found they were never again so much together,
    Divided by the morning tea,
    By the evening paper,
    By children and tradesmen's bills.

Waking at times in the night she found assurance
Due to his regular breathing but wondered whether
  It was really worth it and where
  The river had flowed away
  And where were the white flowers.

Louis MacNeice

LIVE MAN'S EPITAPH

Seeking necessity, he only found
Someone who needed him, and married her.
Having failed to build a house on solid ground
He freely chose the sea, and freely drowned.

Francis Hope

IN THE ROOM OF THE BRIDE-ELECT

'Would it had been the man of our wish!'
Sighs her mother. To whom with vehemence she
In the wedding-dress—the wife to be—
'Then why were you so mollyish
As not to insist on him for me!'
The mother, amazed: 'Why, dearest one
Because you pleaded for this or none!'
'But Father and you should have stood out strong!
Since then, to my cost, I have lived to find
That you were right and that I was wrong;
This man is a dolt to the one declined. . . .
Ah!—here he comes with his button-hole rose.
Good God—I must marry him I suppose!'

Thomas Hardy

THE MAIDENS CAME

The maidens came
When I was in my mother's bower;
I had all that I would.
    The bailey beareth the bell away;
    The lily, the rose, the rose I lay.

The silver is white, red is the gold;
The robes they lay in fold.
    The bailey beareth the bell away;
    The lily, the rose, the rose I lay.

And through the glass window shines the sun.
How should I love, and I so young?
    The bailey beareth the bell away;
    The lily, the rose, the rose I lay.

Anon

WEDDING WIND

The wind blew all my wedding-day,
And my wedding-night was the night of the high
   wind;
And a stable door was banging, again and again,
That he must go and shut it, leaving me
Stupid in candlelight, hearing rain,
Seeing my face in the twisted candlestick,
Yet seeing nothing. When he came back
He said the horses were restless, and I was sad
That any man or beast that night should lack
The happiness I had.

      Now in the day
All's ravelled under the sun by the wind's blowing.
He has gone to look at the floods, and I
Carry a chipped pail to the chicken-run,
Set it down, and stare. All is the wind
Hunting through clouds and forests, thrashing
My apron and the hanging cloths on the line.
Can it be borne, this bodying-forth by wind
Of joy my actions turn on, like a thread
Carrying beads? Shall I be let to sleep
Now this perpetual morning shares my bed?
Can even death dry up
These new delighted lakes, conclude
Our kneeling as cattle by all-generous waters?

Philip Larkin

A SLICE OF WEDDING CAKE

Why have such scores of lovely, gifted girls
   Married impossible men?
Simple self-sacrifice may be ruled out,
   And missionary endeavour, nine times out of ten.

Repeat 'impossible men': not merely rustic,
   Foul-tempered or depraved
(Dramatic foils chosen to show the world
   How well women behave, and always have behaved).

Impossible men: idle, illiterate,
   Self-pitying, dirty, sly,
For whose appearance even in City parks
   Excuses must be made to casual passers-by.

Has God's supply of tolerable husbands
   Fallen, in fact, so low?
Or do I always over-value woman
   At the expense of man?
             Do I?
                It might be so.

Robert Graves

MEDITATION AT KEW

Alas! for all the pretty women who marry dull men,
Go into the suburbs and never come out again,
Who lose their pretty faces, and dim their pretty eyes,
Because no one has skill or courage to organize.

What do these pretty women suffer when they marry?
They bear a boy who is like Uncle Harry,
A girl, who is like Aunt Eliza, and not new.
These old dull races must breed true.

I would enclose a common in the sun,
And let the young wives out to laugh and run;
I would steal their dull clothes and go away,
And leave the pretty naked things to play.

Then I would make a contract with hard Fate
That they see all the men in the world and choose a mate,
And I would summon all the pipers in the town,
That they dance with Love at a feast, and dance him down.

From the gay unions of choice
We'd have a race of splendid beauty, and of thrilling voice.
The World whips frank gay love with rods,
But frankly gaily shall we get the gods.

Anna Wickham

THE FALCON WOMAN

It is hard to be a man
Whose word is his bond
In love with such a woman,

When he builds on a promise
She lightly let fall
In carelessness of spirit.

The more sternly he asks her
To stand by that promise
The faster she flies.

But is it less hard
To be born such a woman
With wings like a falcon
And in carelessness of spirit
To love such a man?

                    Robert Graves

SHE VOWED HIM THIS

Constant I will be
As the tree rooted;

Stitch will I,
Burnish, bake and broom,
And peg the billowing Monday line along
With room for song;

So will my ear
Your day's endeavour praise,
And raise a pillow
For the morrow's care.

Warm will I lie with thee,
So my most pleasure spill
Out of the free, the delicate measure of your will.
This for our seed's sake
And soul's need.

Man, what chances
I will equal share,
Halved grief and double cheer.

As mirrors live,
Toil for your toil, heart for your heart
I give.

William Box

TO MY WIFE

Night still lingers
    in your summer trees

trees that fill your morning window.

Branches sway
    with a hush more soothing
        than silence

lush with cool leaves
    and sleepy sparrows.

Jack Simcock

TO MY WIFE
Sonnet 3

It was a quiet night, you will remember:
warm, with a little mist among the trees;
we had left two children sleeping; the ease
of ten years' loving was between. You were

in a broken mood, remember; I talked
as though I understood the world; the mist
between the trees, concealing lovers, kissed
your mood and pulled your hair uncurled. We walked

where we had been before we married; quiet
it was with my voice droning on; ten years
I talked away before I carried your mood
and you to where the grass was long, and tight
our love became to loose your worries,
as sweet your song becomes when I intrude.

Edwin Brock

THE ALBUM

I see you, a child
In a garden sheltered for buds and playtime,
Listening as if beguiled
By a fancy beyond your years and the flowering maytime.
The print is faded: soon there will be
No trace of that pose enthralling,
Nor visible echo of my voice distantly calling
'Wait! Wait for me!'

Then I turn the page
To a girl who stands like a questioning iris
By the waterside, at an age
That asks every mirror to tell what the heart's desire is.
The answer she finds in that oracle stream
Only time could affirm or disprove,
Yet I wish I was there to venture a warning, 'Love
Is not what you dream.'

Next you appear
As if garlands of wild felicity crowned you—
Courted, caressed, you wear
Like immortelles the lovers and friends around you.
'They will not last you, rain or shine,
They are but straws and shadows,'
I cry: 'Give not to those charming desperadoes
What was made to be mine.'

One picture is missing—
The last. It would show me a tree stripped bare
By intemperate gales, her amazing
Noonday of blossom spoilt which promised so fair.
Yet, scanning those scenes at your heyday taken,
I tremble, as one who must view
In the crystal a doom he could never deflect—yes, I too
Am fruitlessly shaken.

I close the book;
But the past slides out of its leaves to haunt me
And it seems, wherever I look,
Phantoms of irreclaimable happiness taunt me.
Then I see her, petalled in new-blown hours,
Beside me—'All you love most there
Has blossomed again,' she murmurs, 'all that you missed there
Has grown to be yours.'

C. Day Lewis

SONG

Why should a foolish Marriage Vow
   Which long ago was made,
Oblige us to each other now
   When Passion is decay'd?
We lov'd, and we lov'd, as long as we cou'd,
   Till our Love was lov'd out in us both:
But our Marriage is dead, when the Pleasure is
     fled:
   'Twas Pleasure first made it an Oath.

If I have Pleasures for a Friend,
   And farther love in store,
What wrong has he whose joys did end,
   And who cou'd give no more?
'Tis a madness that he should be jealous of me,
   Or that I shou'd bar him of another:
For all we can gain, is to give our selves pain,
   When neither can hinder the other.

John Dryden

THE JUNGLE HUSBAND

Dearest Evelyn, I often think of you
Out with the guns in the jungle stew
Yesterday I hittapotamus
I put the measurements down for you but they got lost in
    the fuss
It's not a good thing to drink out here
You know, I've practically given it up dear.
Tomorrow I am going alone a long way
Into the jungle. It is all grey
But green on top
Only sometimes when a tree has fallen
The sun comes down plop, it is quite appalling.
You never want to go in a jungle pool
In the hot sun, it would be the act of a fool
Because it is always full of anacondas, Evelyn, not looking
                ill-fed
I'll say. So no more now, from your loving husband
              Wilfred.

Stevie Smith

After the First Death, There is No Other

TO LUCASTA
Going to the Warres

Tell me not (Sweet) I am unkinde,
    That from the Nunnerie
Of thy chaste breast, and quiet minde,
    To Warre and Armes I flie.

True; a new Mistresse now I chase,
    The first Foe in the Field;
And with a stronger Faith imbrace
    A Sword, a Horse, a Shield.

Yet this Inconstancy is such,
    As you too shall adore;
I could not love thee (Deare) so much,
    Lov'd I not Honour more.

Richard Lovelace

THE LONG WAR

Less passionate the long war throws
its burning thorn about all men,
caught in one grief, we share one wound,
and cry one dialect of pain.

We have forgot who fired the house,
whose easy mischief spilt first blood,
under one raging roof we lie
the fault no longer understood.

But as our twisted arms embrace
the desert where our cities stood,
death's family likeness in each face
must show, at last, our brotherhood.

Laurie Lee

WAR POET

I am the man who looked for peace and found
My own eyes barbed.
I am the man who groped for words and found
An arrow in my hand.
I am the builder whose firm walls surround
A slipping land.
When I grow sick or mad
Mock me not nor chain me:
When I reach for the wind
Cast me not down:
Though my face is a burnt book
And a wasted town.

Sidney Keyes

IS THERE NO LOVE CAN LINK US?

Is there no thread to bind us—I and he
Who is dying now, this instant as I write
And may be cold before this line's complete?

Is there no power to link us—I and she
Across whose body the loud roof is falling?

Or the child, whose blackening skin
Blossoms with hideous roses in the smoke?

Is there no love can link us—I and they?
Only this hectic moment? This fierce instant
Striking now
Its universal, its uneven blow?

There is no other link. Only this sliding
Second we share: this desperate edge of now.

Mervyn Peake

A REFUSAL TO MOURN THE DEATH, BY FIRE, OF A CHILD IN LONDON

Never until the mankind making
Bird beast and flower
Fathering and all humbling darkness
Tells with silence the last light breaking
And the still hour
Is come of the sea tumbling in harness

And I must enter again the round
Zion of the water bead
And the synagogue of the ear of corn
Shall I let pray the shadow of a sound
Or sow my salt seed
In the least valley of sackcloth to mourn

The majesty and burning of the child's death.
I shall not murder
The mankind of her going with a grave truth
Nor blaspheme down the stations of the breath
With any further
Elegy of innocence and youth.

Deep with the first dead lies London's daughter,
Robed in the long friends,
The grains beyond age, the dark veins of her mother,
Secret by the unmourning water
Of the riding Thames.
After the first death, there is no other.

Dylan Thomas

FIVE MINUTES AFTER THE AIR RAID

In Pilsen,
Twenty-six Station Road,
she climbed to the Third Floor
up stairs which were all that was left
of the whole house,
she opened her door
full on to the sky,
stood gaping over the edge.

For this was the place
the world ended.

Then
she locked up carefully
lest someone steal
Sirius
or Aldebaran
from her kitchen,
went back downstairs
and settled herself
to wait
for the house to rise again
and for her husband to rise from the ashes
and for her children's hands and feet to be stuck
    back in place.

In the morning they found her
still as stone,
sparrows pecking her hands.

Miroslav Holub

ANTHEM FOR DOOMED YOUTH

What passing-bells for these who die as cattle?
   Only the monstrous anger of the guns.
   Only the stuttering rifles' rapid rattle
Can patter out their hasty orisons.
No mockeries for them from prayers or bells,
   Nor any voice of mourning save the choirs,—
The shrill, demented choirs of wailing shells;
   And bugles calling for them from sad shires.

What candles may be held to speed them all?
   Not in the hands of boys, but in their eyes
Shall shine the holy glimmers of good-byes.
   The pallor of girls' brows shall be their pall;
Their flowers the tenderness of silent minds,
And each slow dusk a drawing-down of blinds.

Wilfred Owen

THE EFFECT

'*The effect of our bombardment was terrific. One man told me he had never seen so many dead before.*'—War Correspondent.

'*He'd never seen so many dead before.*'
They sprawled in yellow daylight while he swore
And gasped and lugged his everlasting load
Of bombs along what once had been a road.
'*How peaceful are the dead.*'
Who put that silly gag in some one's head?

'*He'd never seen so many dead before.*'
The lilting words danced up and down his brain,
While corpses jumped and capered in the rain.
No, no; he wouldn't count them any more . . .
The dead have done with pain:
They've choked; they can't come back to life again.

When Dick was killed last week he looked like that,
Flapping along the fire-step like a fish,
After the blazing crump had knocked him flat . . .
'*How many dead? As many as ever you wish.
Don't count 'em; they're too many.
Who'll buy my nice fresh corpses, two a penny?*'

Siegfried Sassoon

BROKEN PROMISE
To Siegfried Sassoon (d. 1967)

Now you are dead
Those years under the fleeing skies of France
Seem buried with you.
Fifty years of lies and laughter have dulled
The heavy impact of the guns.
The torn helmets are rusting in Bethune,
And the mud has closed up long ago
So go now.

The voices of the dead
Were all your life, the drowning, cursing
Screams forced out your words though
Our laughter must have seemed bayonets
Struck through their gullets.
And now you're gone it's strange
Death came so late
We turned against the dead so soon

Remembrance Day rings hollow
As the skulls at Mons.

James O. Taylor

GOD BLESS U S

dreaming
I saw a butterfly in the night
yellow bright and beautiful
I watched you call it red and watched you crush it
and all I did was to get up
and wash my face

awake
I listen to old jazz
soul jazz
and dig the strokes
the sharp edge of the penetrating steel
awake
I listen to same home steel
digging through Vietcongs
and all I did was to get up
and wash my face

watching
you soul brother
having heard your wail in Mississippi
watching you rot in mother Harlem
noting your bullets whizzing through your yellow brother
and the tattoo on your heroic skin
god bless U S
I might as well get up again
and wash my eyes and ears

Gaston Bart-Williams

'HE KILLED MANY OF MY MEN'

(from the photograph of Brigadier Nguyen Ngoc Loan summarily executing a Vietcong officer)

          this morning
a gun held at a man's ear
what comforting words did it
whisper to him,
before it killed him in the middle
of a dry street
          words of vengeance
did it whisper that the finger that crooked
for him crooked for a hundred others
          that his blood will mix
with American blood on the dog's tongue
walking carelessly upon the bullets
          the burning lens of a
world will focus on the executioner's
forehead
          the hatred will be
carried, the flame given out of hand
into hand
          will complete the circle,
passed into a camera carried over the
cables into England
          a man in a check
shirt with his eyes fixed on me and his

hair blown in a last wind, so now
when the wind blows in my hair do
I open my fist for the spark
                              or whisper derisive
comforts in my ear

John Bennett

FUTILITY

Move him into the sun—
Gently its touch awoke him once,
At home, whispering of fields unsown.
Always it woke him, even in France,
Until this morning and this snow.
If anything might rouse him now
The kind old sun will know.

Think how it wakes the seeds,—
Woke, once, the clays of a cold star.
Are limbs, so dear-achieved, are sides,
Full-nerved—still warm—too hard to stir?
Was it for this the clay grew tall?
—O what made fatuous sunbeams toil
To break earth's sleep at all?

Wilfred Owen

THE END OF LOVE

Now he is dead
How should I know
My true love's arms
From wind and snow?

No man I meet
In field or house,
Though in the street
A hundred pass.

The hurrying dust
Has never a face,
No longer human
In man or woman.

Now he is gone
Why should I mourn
My true love more
Than mud or stone?

Kathleen Raine

CHRISTMAS: 1924

'Peace upon earth!' was said. We sing it,
And pay a million priests to bring it.
After two thousand years of mass
We've got as far as poison gas.

Thomas Hardy

NOON HOUR

Noon-hour

and the children come in
like wind
wild at the door,
blowing the stale
and dusty world

they charge me,
the morning at school
pitched like a javelin
into the cave.

'Look, mummy!
We had Civil Defence today!
They showed us how to do this—

Isn't it funny?'

And they go into Arab positions
of prayer on the floor,
the little snow-flakes
of their hands,
clasped tight behind their heads,
elbows tucked in about their ears,
bottoms in the air.

'You should get near a wall.'

'This is to protect the jugular veins.'

They give a giggling good
description
of flying glass
fashioned into daggers

And my little one comes in
from the end of her record,
'Here we go round the mulberry bush',
quickly joins her brothers
in their game,
curling into a little laughing
doom-ball on the floor.

(Yes, I suppose that is as idiotic
a position as any—
putting one's back to it
and shutting one's eyes;
make it acceptable
by pretending there is
a defence—)

Oh, never was Woman so cold and small
in the steam-kettle mists
of the children
gone back to school

But I must do more than wring
my hands.

Joan Finnigan

MOTHER THE WARDROBE IS FULL OF INFANTRYMEN

mother the wardrobe is full of infantrymen
i did i asked them
but they snarled saying it was a mans life

mother there is a centurian tank in the parlour
i did i asked the officer
but he laughed saying 'Queens regulations'
(piano was out of tune anyway)

mother polish your identity bracelet
there is a mushroom cloud in the backgarden
i did i tried to bring in the cat
but it simply came to pieces in my hand
i did i tried to whitewash the windows
but there weren't any
i did i tried to hide under the stairs
but i couldn't get in for civil defence leaders
i did i tried ringing candid camera
but they crossed their hearts

i went for a policeman but they were looting the town
i went out for a fire engine but they were all upside down
i went for a priest but they were all on their knees
mother don't just lie there say something please
mother don't just lie there say something please

Roger McGough

117

A CHILD IS SINGING

A child is singing
And nobody listening
But the child who is singing:

Bulldozers grab the earth and shower it.
The house is on fire.
Gardeners wet the earth and flower it.
The house is on fire,
The houses are on fire.
Fetch the fire engine, the fire engine's on fire.
We will have to hide in a hole.
We will burn slow like coal.
All the people are on fire

And a child is singing
And nobody listening
But the child who is singing.

Adrian Mitchell

RELATIVE SADNESS

Einstein's eyes
were filled with tears
when he heard about Hiroshima.
Mr. Tamiki
had no eyes left
to show his grief.

Colin Rowbotham

OUR FEAR

Our fear
does not wear a night shirt
does not have owl's eyes
does not lift a casket lid
does not extinguish a candle

does not have a dead man's face either

our fear
is a scrap of paper
found in a pocket
'warn Wójcik
the place on Dluga Street is hot'

our fear
does not rise on the wings of the tempest
does not sit on a church tower
it is down-to-earth

it has the shape
of a bundle made in haste
with warm clothing
provisions
and arms

our fear
does not have the face of a dead man
the dead are gentle to us
we carry them on our shoulders
sleep under the same blanket

close their eyes
adjust their lips
pick a dry spot
and bury them

not too deep
not too shallow

Zbigniew Herbert

A HOPE FOR THOSE SEPARATED BY WAR

They crossed her face with blood,
They hung her heart.
They dragged her through a pit
Full of quick sorrow.
Yet her small feet
Ran back on the morrow.

They took his book and caged
His mind in a dark house.
They took his bright eyes
To light their rooms of doubt.
Yet his thin hands
Crawled back and found her out.

Sidney Keyes

THIRD DEGREE

Hit me! Jab me!
Make me say I did it.
Blood on my sport shirt
And my tan suede shoes.

Faces like jack-o'-lanterns
In gray slouch hats.

Slug me! Beat me!
Scream jumps out
Like blow-torch.
Three kicks between the legs
That kill the kids
I'd make tomorrow.

Bars and floor skyrocket
And burst like Roman candles.

When you throw
Cold water on me,
I'll sign the
Paper. . . .

                    Langston Hughes

LEAVE US ALONE

Forget about us
about our generation
live like human beings
forget about us

we envied
plants and stones
we envied dogs

I would like to be a rat
I used to say to her

I would like not to be
I would like to fall asleep
and wake up after the war
she would say with her eyes shut

forget about us
don't ask about our youth
leave us alone

Tadeusz Rozewicz

SOMEONE IS BEATING A WOMAN

Someone is beating a woman.
In the car that is dark and hot
Only the whites of her eyes shine.
Her legs thrash against the roof
Like berserk searchlight beams.

Someone is beating a woman.
This is the way slaves are beaten.
Frantic, she wrenches open the door
And plunges out—onto the road.

Brakes scream.
Someone runs up to her,
Strikes her and drags her, face down,
In the grass lashing with nettles.

Scum, how meticulously he beats her,
Stilyaga, bastard, big hero,
His smart flatiron-pointed shoe
Stabbing into her ribs.

Such are the pleasures of enemy soldiers
And the brute refinements of peasants.
Trampling underfoot the moonlit grass,
Someone is beating a woman.

Someone is beating a woman.
Century on century, no end to this.

It's the young that are beaten. Somberly
Our wedding bells start up the alarum.
Someone is beating a woman.

What about the flaming weals
In the braziers of their cheeks?
That's life, you say. Are you telling me?
Someone is beating a woman.

But her light is unfaltering
World-without-ending.
There are no religions,
                              no revelations,
There are women.

Lying there pale as water
Her eyes tear-closed and still,
She doesn't belong to him
Any more than a meadow deep in a wood.

And the stars? Rattling in the sky
Like raindrops against black glass,
Plunging down,
                    they cool
Her grief-fevered forehead.

Andrei Voznesensky

A HISTORY LESSON

Kings
like golden gleams
made with a mirror on the wall.

A non-alcoholic pope,
knights without arms,
arms without knights.

The dead like so many strained noodles,
a pound of those fallen in battle,
two ounces of those who were executed,

several heads
like so many potatoes
shaken into a cap—

Geniuses conceived
by the mating of dates
are soaked up by the ceiling into infinity

to the sound of tinny thunder,
the rumble of bellies,
shouts of hurrah,

empires rise and fall
at a wave of the pointer,
the blood is blotted out—

And only one small boy,
who was not paying the least attention,
will ask
between two victorious wars:

And did it hurt in those days too?

Miroslav Holub

NO MATTER IF YOU REMAIN UNAFFECTED BY

No matter if you remain unaffected by
that animal that makes wars
and sends the smallest child to slaughter
I recognize your shape however sacred burns
and deeper than the lyric bird
lies one dark and gibbering.

And though love sings from a separate source than makes wars
the heart's easily shattered
and pure miracles that once danced through air and frozen time
drain to places where we cannot follow
and love goes limping with its sores.
Our shapes will not stand against the smallest bombs.

As a rabbit stunned by light was I by beauty,
sat glittering inside myself while through the world
deep dwarfs came swarming
and climbed into my dreams—

There are good explosions, but they grow scarce
and deeper than the lyric bird
lies one dark and gibbering.

Brian Patten

April Comes Like an Idiot

SPRING

To what purpose, April, do you return again?
Beauty is not enough.
You can no longer quiet me with the redness
Of little leaves opening stickily.
I know what I know.
The sun is hot on my neck as I observe
The spikes of the crocus.
The smell of the earth is good.
It is apparent that there is no death.
But what does that signify?
Not only under ground are the brains of men
Eaten by maggots.
Life in itself
Is nothing,
An empty cup, a flight of uncarpeted stairs.
It is not enough that yearly, down this hill,
April
Comes like an idiot, babbling and strewing flowers.

Edna St. Vincent Millay

THE UNKNOWN CITIZEN
(To JS/07/M/378 This Marble Monument is Erected by the State)

He was found by the Bureau of Statistics to be
One against whom there was no official complaint,
And all the reports on his conduct agree
That, in the modern sense of an old-fashioned word, he was
    a saint,
For in everything he did he served the Greater Community.
Except for the War till the day he retired
He worked in a factory and never got fired,
But satisfied his employers, Fudge Motors Inc.
Yet he wasn't a scab or odd in his views,
For his Union reports that he paid his dues,
(Our report on his Union shows it was sound)
And our Social Psychology workers found
That he was popular with his mates and liked a drink.
The Press are convinced that he bought a paper every day
And that his reactions to advertisements were normal in
    every way.
Policies taken out in his name prove that he was fully
    insured,
And his Health-card shows he was once in hospital but left
    it cured.
Both Producers Research and High-Grade Living declare
He was fully sensible to the advantages of the Instalment Plan
And had everything necessary to the Modern Man,
A phonograph, a radio, a car and a frigidaire.

Our researchers into Public Opinion are content
That he held the proper opinions for the time of year;
When there was peace, he was for peace; when there was
    war, he went.
He was married and added five children to the population,
Which our Eugenist says was the right number for a parent of his
    generation,
And our teachers report he never interfered with their education.
Was he free? Was he happy? The question is absurd:
Had anything been wrong, we should certainly have heard.

W. H. Auden

THE MAN IN THE BOWLER HAT

I am the unnoticed, the unnoticeable man:
The man who sat on your right in the morning train:
The man you looked through like a windowpane:
The man who was the colour of the carriage, the colour
   of the mounting
Morning pipe smoke.

I am the man too busy with a living to live,
Too hurried and worried to see and smell and touch:
The man who is patient too long and obeys too much
And wishes too softly and seldom.

I am the man they call the nation's backbone,
Who am boneless—playable catgut, pliable clay:
The Man they label Little lest one day
I dare to grow.

I am the rails on which the moment passes,
The megaphone for many words and voices:
I am graph, diagram,
Composite face.

I am the led, the easily-fed,
The tool, the not-quite-fool,
The would-be-safe-and-sound,
The uncomplaining bound,
The dust fine-ground,
Stone-for-a-statue waveworn pebble-round.

Peter Black

135

THE MAN ON MY BACK

The man on my back
Hates my guts,
Gives me no rest
And spurns all I love best.

The man on my back
Tears my dreams apart
And ravages my heart;
Give him enough rope
He'll strangle every hope.

The man on my back,
He's a killer—
Kills the boy in me,
And the man that would be;
The man on my back,
My replica.

Pradip Sen

LOOKING UP

Looking up
Up above me
I hear screams
Screams of fear
Screams of nothing
Nothing just like me
For I am nowhere
I am here
Screaming Screaming.

John Allcock

IS THERE ANY REWARD?

Is there any reward?
   I'm beginning to doubt it.
I am broken and bored,
   Is there any reward?
Reassure me, Good Lord,
   And inform me about it,
Is there any reward?
   I'm beginning to doubt it.

Hilaire Belloc

LOVE SONG: I AND THOU

Nothing is plumb, level or square:
    the studs are bowed, the joists
are shaky by nature, no piece fits
    any other piece without a gap
or pinch, and bent nails
    dance all over the surfacing
like maggots. By Christ
    I am no carpenter. I built
the roof for myself, the walls
    for myself, the floors
for myself, and got
    hung up in it myself. I
danced with a purple thumb
    at this house-warming, drunk
with my prime whiskey: rage.
    Oh I spat rage's nails
into the frame-up of my work:
    it held. It settled plumb,
level, solid, square and true
    for that great moment. Then
it screamed and went on through,
    skewing as wrong the other way.
God damned it. This is hell,
    but I planned it, I sawed it,
I nailed it, and I
    will live in it until it kills me.

I can nail my left palm
	to the left-hand cross-piece but
I can't do everything myself.
	I need a hand to nail the right,
a help, a love, a you, a wife.

Alan Dugan

LITTLE JOHNNY'S FOOLISH INVENTION
A Fable for Atomic Adam

One day
    while playing with old junk in the attic
    Little Johnny accidentally invented an atomic bomb
    and not knowing what to do with it
    buried it in the front garden.

Next morning
    during cornflakes and sunrise
    he noticed it glowing damp among the cabbages
    and so took it out
    out into the city
    where it smelt of tulips
    but was sadly inedible.

What can I do with it, he sighed, having nowhere to hide it?
I'm afraid that soon a busy policeman might come along
to detain me. I'd make a statement. Say

        I'd like a new bomb, a blue bomb,
a bomb I could explode in dormitories
where my friends are sleeping,
that would not wake them or shake them but
would simply keep them from weeping;
        a bomb I could bounce in the playground
and spray over flowers, a bomb
that would light the Universe for years and send down
showers of joy.

But he'd pay no attention he
would simply take out his notebook and write:
This child is mad.
This child is a bomb.

*   *   *

Last night in my nightmares
the bomb became transparent
and through it my atomic friends wandered, naked
but for a few carefully placed leaves
that were continually rotting.

So now looking much older
I trace about obscure cities
looking for a place to leave my bomb
but am always turned away by minor officials
who say, 'It's a deterrent,' and I answer, 'Sure!'

It will deter
flowers and birds and the sunlight from calling
and one morning
at sunrise when I rise and glow
I'll look outside to make certain my invention has not
bloomed
but will see nothing through
the melting windows.

Brian Patten

White Against Dawn

I AM THE GREAT SUN
(from a Normandy crucifix of 1632)

I am the great sun, but you do not see me,
  I am your husband, but you turn away.
I am the captive, but you do not free me,
  I am the captain you will not obey.

I am the truth, but you will not believe me,
  I am the city where you will not stay,
I am your wife, your child, but you will leave me,
  I am that God to whom you will not pray.

I am your counsel, but you do not hear me,
  I am the lover whom you will betray,
I am the victor, but you do not cheer me,
  I am the holy dove whom you will slay.

  I am your life, but if you will not name me,
  Seal up your soul with tears, and never blame me.

Charles Causley

145

HEAVEN-HAVEN
A Nun Takes the Veil

I have desired to go
   Where springs not fail,
To fields where flies no sharp and sided hail
   And a few lilies blow.

And I have asked to be
   Where no storms come,
Where the green swell is in the havens dumb,
   And out of the swing of the sea.

Gerard Manley Hopkins

MYTHISTOREMA
XXIII

Just a little more
And we shall see the almond trees in blossom
The marbles shining in the sun
The sea, the curling waves.

Just a little more
Let us rise just a little higher.

George Seferis

GIVE ME PEACE

Give me quietness and peace . . .
My nerves are badly burnt, I guess,
give me peace . . .

       Let the pine tree slowly shift
its shadow which tickles us as it goes
down our backs all the way to our toes
with a kind of cooling mischief.
Give us peace . . .

All sounds have ceased.
Why put in words the iridescence
of your eyebrows? You nod in silence.
Give us peace.

Sound travels much slower
than light: let's give our tongues a rest
—in any case, essentials are nameless,
better rely on feeling and color.

The skin is also human, dear,
with sensations peculiar to it:
a finger's touch is music to it,
like a nightingale's song to the ear.

What's with you windbags back at home?
Still shouting blue murder and fussing?
Still raising hell about nothing?
Leave us alone . . .

. . . we're deep in something else,
immersed in nature's inscrutable ways.
From an acrid smell of smoke we surmise
that the shepherds are back from the hills.

It's dusk. They're cooking their suppers
and smoking, each as hushed as his shadow,
and like flames of cigarette lighters
the silent tongues of sheep dogs glow.

Andrei Voznesensky

ODE TO JOY

You only love
when you love in vain.

Try another radio probe
when ten have failed,
take two hundred rabbits
when a hundred have died:
only this is science.

You ask the secret.
It has just one name:
again.

In the end
a dog carries in his jaws
his image in the water,
people rivet the new moon,
I love you.

Like caryatids
our lifted arms
hold up time's granite load

and defeated
we shall always win.

Miroslav Holub

STILL HERE

I've been scarred and battered.
My hopes the wind done scattered.
Snow has friz me, sun has baked me.
  Looks like between 'em
  They done tried to make me
Stop laughin', stop lovin', stop livin'—
  But I don't care!
  I'm still here!

Langston Hughes

WHAT YOU SHOULD DO EACH MORNING

At last it cannot matter
what openings are seen through
as long as outside any are

the same still horses, poised
against dawn, so
very white against dawn:

it does not matter
as long as shouting Yes
you rush outside

leaping on any of them then
ride madly away
singing, singing, singing.

Brian Patten

The Day Waits

SUMMER SOLSTICE

The mountain's green and shining
And white rocks at the top.
It's the longest day of the year.
It'll never be lighter than this.

I climb in good boots,
Sure on the slopes,
Proof against wind
And bright against loss,
(These anoraks can be seen at a mile).

Behind me the sun slips.
I climb fast.
It's the longest day of the year.
The mountain's purple, and I reach
The black rocks at the top.
I mean well,
But I can't climb faster
Than the world turns.
It'll never be lighter than this.

Alan Garner

STILL BRANCHES

The day waits quietly
as though nothing has ever happened before
as though all that will happen today
will be for the first time.

In still branches the day waits.

I wake without memory
without anticipation
I wake with closed eyes
from an ecstasy of pining
unrequited love long ago
weak from a boy's heart
broken for life in dreams.

First love is lost and sought in dreams tearfully.
The pleading is remembered
lived with
Morning is to accept the loss.

I rise and go about my day
and again everything is old
and I do everything the way I always do it
I say again what I said yesterday
and everything I see I remember
and everything is saturated in the past.

The day waits quietly to be remembered.

Soon I am of yesterday and to the future.

I rise from a burden of ills
to a burden of desires
I embrace each new day
and it dies in my arms
the same death as yesterday.

I pass narrowly through a jungle of temptation
Torments litter my way
The blizzard of life piles me with beauty
It crowds my days
Grazes my eyes
Lines my way from place to place from room to room
The agony is the inevitable loss

I am buried in change
alive and untidy
Every day reveals more life to lose
                    more loss to grieve
                    more death to fear.
The night whispers the truth.

I sleep for tomorrow.

Jack Simcock

A NIGHT OUT

Friends recommended the new Polish film
at the Academy in Oxford Street.
So we joined the ever melancholy queue
of cinemas. A wind blew faint suggestions
of rain towards us, and an accordion.
Later, uneasy, in the velvet dark
we peered through the cut-out, oblong window
at the spotlit drama of our nightmares:
images of Auschwitz almost authentic,
the human obscenity in close-up.
Certainly we could imagine the stench.

Resenting it, we forgot the barbed wire
was but a prop, and could not scratch an eye:
those striped victims merely actors, like us.
We saw the Camp orchestra assembled,
we heard the solemn gaiety of Bach,
scored by the loud arrival of an engine,
its impotent cry, and its guttural trucks.
We watched, as we munched milk chocolate,
trustful children, no older than our own,
strolling into the chambers without fuss,
whilst smoke, black and curly, oozed from chimneys.

Afterwards, at a loss, we sipped coffee
in a bored espresso bar near by
saying very little. You took off one glove.

Then to the comfortable suburb swiftly
where, arriving home, we garaged the car.
We asked the au pair girl from Germany
if anyone had phoned at all, or called,
and, of course, if the children had woken.
Reassured, together we climbed the stairs,
undressed together, and naked together,
in the dark, in the marital bed, made love.

Dannie Abse

DO NOT DREAM

Do not dream. Dangerous dreams mark
a limit a man might not
dream beyond. Dangerous dreams.

Do not dream.
Philosophers regard the whole
world as dream. The mother lulls
her son to sleep. Dream is
what creeps from a mother
lulling her son to sleep.

Do not dream. Unavoidable
dreams infiltrate our thoughts;
guests, uninvited. Distorted dreams
conflict our youth, teach us, the old, age.
Terrible dreams force

upon the righteous, glory; upon the forgotten, forgetfulness;
upon the malicious, their malice; to each man
whom time has passed like evil waters, a seal.

Natan Zach

BEDTIME STORY FOR MY SON

Where did the voice come from? I hunted through the rooms
For that small boy, that high, that head-voice,
The clatter as his heels caught on the door,
A shadow just caught moving through the door
Something like a school-satchel. My wife
Didn't seem afraid, even when it called for food
She smiled and turned her book and said:
'I couldn't go and love the empty air.'

We went to bed. Our dreams seemed full
Of boys in one or another guise, the paper-boy
Skidding along in grubby jeans, a music-lesson
She went out in the early afternoon to fetch a child from.
I pulled up from a pillow damp with heat
And saw her kissing hers, her legs were folded
Far away from mine. A pillow! It seemed
She couldn't love the empty air.

Perhaps, we thought, a child had come to grief
In some room in the old house we kept,
And listened if the noises came from some especial room,
And then we'd take the boards up and discover
A pile of dusty bones like charcoal twigs and give
The tiny-sounding ghost a proper resting-place
So that it need not wander in the empty air.

No blood-stained attic harboured the floating sounds,
We found they came in rooms that we'd warmed with our life.

We traced the voice and found where it mostly came
From just underneath both our skins, and not only
In the night-time either, but at the height of noon
And when we sat at meals alone. Plainly, this is how we found
That love pines loudly to go out to where
It need not spend itself on fancy and the empty air.

Peter Redgrove

CROWSFEET SPLAYING ROUND HIS EYES

Crowsfeet splaying round his eyes
And laughter in them.
Bending over a grandchild, patting a head,
And sixpence to spend.

Not *his* grandchild. And sadness clouds the laughter.
The crowsfeet fly away to some place
Where.

Back to a small, gas-undarkened, gas-unfrozen room
And another term of loneliness.

Silence now.

But awake to a bright, bird-singing morning
And once more a walk to a seat in the park.

Wait through afternoon. Then the mothers come
With children, and the cycle starts again
Of once more gladness, crowsfeet, laughter unsounded.

And one more reason for some hope,
Another head to pat, another smile,
Another comfort.
Another day.

L. Paul Lloyd-Evans

THE CHILD UNBORN

There is a child unborn
in the face of
all women, even the old
who have outworn
childbearing and love.
It is the tale untold
of the unslakeable thirst
dimly imagined
in the heart foredoomed to carry
unfulfilment from the first.
It is the legend
of Mary
waiting for the angel, who
cometh not at dusk
or at morn.
In the face of all of you,
women, I see the death-mask
of a world unborn.

Humbert Wolfe

A MAD POEM ADDRESSED TO MY NEPHEWS AND NIECES

The World cheats those who cannot read;
I, happily, have mastered script and pen.
The World cheats those who hold no office;
I am blessed with high official rank.
The old are often ill;
I, at this day have not an ache or pain.
They are often burdened with ties;
But *I* have finished with marriage and giving in marriage.
No changes happen to jar the quiet of my mind;
No business comes to impair the vigour of my limbs.
Hence it is that now for ten years
Body and soul have rested in hermit peace.
And all the more, in the last lingering years
What I shall need are very few things.
A single rug to warm me through the winter;
One meal to last me the whole day.
It does not matter that my house is rather small;
One cannot sleep in more than one room!
It does not matter that I have not many horses;
One cannot ride in two coaches at once!
As fortunate as me among the people of the world
Possibly one would find seven out of ten.
As contented as me among a hundred men
Look as you may, you will not find one.
In the affairs of others even fools are wise;
In their own business even sages err.
To no one else would I dare to speak my heart.
So my wild words are addressed to my nephews and nieces.

Po Chü-i

OLD WOMAN

So much she caused she cannot now account for
As she stands watching day return, the cool
Walls of the house moving towards the sun.
She puts some flowers in a vase and thinks
   'There is not much I can arrange
In here and now, but flowers are suppliant

As children never were. And love is now
A flicker of memory, my body is
My own entirely. When I lie at night
I gather nothing now into my arms,
   No child or man, and where I live
Is what remains when men and children go.'

Yet she owns more than residue of lives
That she has marked and altered. See how she
Warns time from too much touching her possessions
   By keeping flowers fed, by polishing
     Her fine old silver. Gratefully
She sees her own glance printed on grandchildren.

Drawing the curtains back and opening windows
Every morning now, she feels her years
Grow less and less. Time puts no burden on
Her now she does not need to measure it.
     It is acceptance she arranges
And her own life she places in the vase.

Elizabeth Jennings

EVEN SUCH IS TYME

These verses following were made by Sir Walter Ralegh the night before he dyed and left att the Gate howse.

Even such is tyme which takes in trust
Our yowth, our Ioyes, and all we have,
And payes us butt with age and dust:
Who in the darke and silent grave
When we have wandred all our wayes
Shutts up the storye of our dayes.
And from which earth and grave and dust
The Lord shall rayse me up I trust.

Sir Walter Ralegh

A Handfulla Stars

LET ME DIE A YOUNGMAN'S DEATH

Let me die a youngman's death
not a clean & inbetween
the sheets holywater death
not a famous-last-words
peaceful out of breath death

When I'm 73
& in constant good tumour
may I be mown down at dawn
by a bright red sports car
on my way home
from an allnight party

Or when I'm 91
with silver hair
& sitting in a barber's chair
may rival gangsters
with hamfisted tommyguns burst in
& give me a short back & insides

Or when I'm 104
& banned from the Cavern
may my mistress
catching me in bed with her daughter
& fearing her son
cut me up into little pieces
& throw away every piece but one

Let me die a youngman's death
not a free from sin tiptoe in
candle wax & waning death
not a curtains drawn by angels borne
'what a nice way to go' death

Roger McGough

DO NOT GO GENTLE INTO THAT GOOD NIGHT

Do not go gentle into that good night,
Old age should burn and rave at close of day;
Rage, rage against the dying of the light.

Though wise men at their end know dark is right,
Because their words had forked no lightning they
Do not go gentle into that good night.

Good men, the last wave by, crying how bright
Their frail deeds might have danced in a green bay,
Rage, rage against the dying of the light.

Wild men who caught and sang the sun in flight,
And learn, too late, they grieved it on its way,
Do not go gentle into that good night.

Grave men, near death, who see with blinding sight
Blind eyes could blaze like meteors and be gay,
Rage, rage against the dying of the light.

And you, my father, there on the sad height,
Curse, bless, me now with your fierce tears, I pray.
Do not go gentle into that good night.
Rage, rage against the dying of the light.

Dylan Thomas

A SONG FOR SIMEON

Lord, the Roman hyacinths are blooming in bowls and
The winter sun creeps by the snow hills;
The stubborn season has made stand.
My life is light, waiting for the death wind,
Like a feather on the back of my hand.
Dust in sunlight and memory in corners
Wait for the wind that chills towards the dead land.

   Grant us thy peace.
I have walked many years in this city,
Kept faith and fast, provided for the poor,
Have given and taken honour and ease.
There went never any rejected from my door.
Who shall remember my house, where shall live my
   children's children
When the time of sorrow is come?
They will take to the goat's path, and the fox's home,
Fleeing from the foreign faces and the foreign swords.

   Before the time of cords and scourges and lamentation
Grant us thy peace.
Before the stations of the mountain of desolation,
Before the certain hour of maternal sorrow,
Now at this birth season of decease,
Let the Infant, the still unspeaking and unspoken Word,
Grant Israel's consolation
   To one who has eighty years and no to-morrow.

According to thy word.
They shall praise Thee and suffer in every generation
With glory and derision,
Light upon light, mounting the saints' stair.
Not for me the martyrdom, the ecstasy of thought and
    prayer,
Not for me the ultimate vision.
Grant me thy peace.
(And a sword shall pierce thy heart,
Thine also).
I am tired with my own life and the lives of those after me,
I am dying in my own death and the deaths of those after
    me.
Let thy servant depart,
Having seen thy salvation.

T. S. Eliot

DEATH IS A DOOR

Death is a door
A big black door
No key
No handle
Just a big black door.

John Allcock

HEH NONNY NO!

Heh nonny no!
Men are fools that wish to die!
Is't not fine to dance and sing
When the bells of death do ring?
Is't not fine to swim in wine,
And turn upon the toe
And sing hey nonny no,
When the winds blow and the seas flow?
Hey nonny no!

Anon

AMERICAN GOTHIC
TO SATCH

Sometimes I feel like I will *never* stop
Just go on forever
'Til one fine mornin'
I'm gonna reach up and grab me a handfulla stars
Swing out my long lean leg
And whip three hot strikes burnin' down the heavens
And look over at God and say
How about that!

Samuel Allen (Paul Vesey)

LIFE ROUNDED WITH SLEEP

The babe is at peace within the womb;
The corpse is at rest within the tomb:
  We begin in what we end.

Percy Bysshe Shelley

Prayer Before Birth

PRAYER BEFORE BIRTH

I am not yet born; O hear me.
Let not the bloodsucking bat or the rat or the stoat or the
   clubfooted ghoul come near me.

I am not yet born; console me.
I fear that the human race may with tall walls wall me,
   with strong drugs dope me, with wise lies lure me,
      on black racks rack me, in blood-baths roll me.

I am not yet born; provide me
With water to dandle me, grass to grow for me, trees to talk
   to me, sky to sing to me, birds and a white light
      in the back of my mind to guide me.

I am not yet born; forgive me
For the sins that in me the world shall commit, my words
   when they speak me, my thoughts when they think me,
      my treason engendered by traitors beyond me,
         my life when they murder by means of my
            hands, my death when they live me.

I am not yet born; rehearse me
In the parts I must play and the cues I must take when
   old men lecture me, bureaucrats hector me, mountains
      frown at me, lovers laugh at me, the white
         waves call me to folly and the desert calls
           me to doom and the beggar refuses
              my gift and my children curse me.

I am not yet born; O hear me,
Let not the man who is beast or who thinks he is God
        come near me.

I am not yet born; O fill me
With strength against those who would freeze my
        humanity, would dragoon me into a lethal automaton,
            would make me a cog in a machine, a thing with
                one face, a thing, and against all those
                    who would dissipate my entirety, would
                        blow me like thistledown hither and
                            thither or hither and thither
                                like water held in the
                                    hands would spill me.
Let them not make me a stone and let them not spill me.
Otherwise kill me.

Louis MacNeice

Notes

1 *DIGGING FOR CHINA: Richard Wilbur.* (p. 11)
A paten is a plate used for the bread in the Eucharist.

2 *LA FIGLIA CHE PIANGE: T. S. Eliot.* (p. 44)
The title, in Italian, means 'The Weeping Girl'.
The Latin, 'O quam te memorem virgo . . .' means 'Oh, you will linger in my memory.'

3 *BECAUSE I BREATHE NOT LOVE TO EVERY ONE: Sir Philip Sidney.* (p. 55)
The poet is questioning the convention of his time, which expected certain behaviour from people in love. He says that true love is so overwhelming that it has no words—a concept expressed by Ted Hughes four hundred years later in his PARLOUR PIECE. (p. 56)

4 *SOMEONE IS BEATING A WOMAN: Andrei Voznesensky.* (p. 125)
Stilyaga, literally translated means 'stylist'. It is a derogatory term used to label young Russians who, because they imitate Western fashions, are thought to be particularly decadent. It is intended to express the distaste of older people, just as 'mod', 'rocker', 'skinhead' or 'hippie' are often used here.

5 *EVEN SUCH IS TYME: Sir Walter Ralegh.* (p. 167)
This poem was found in Sir Walter Ralegh's bible in the Gatehouse at Westminster after his execution.

6 *LET ME DIE A YOUNGMAN'S DEATH: Roger McGough.* (p. 171)
The Cavern is the basement club in Liverpool where The Beatles were 'discovered'.

Acknowledgements

The Editor and Publishers are grateful to the following copyright holders for permission to include copyright material in this anthology:

For DANNIE ABSE: 'A Night Out' from *A Small Desperation*; to Hutchinson Publishing Co. Ltd., London, and Christy & Moore Ltd., and Oxford University Press, New York.

For BELLA AKHMADULINA: 'Fifteen Boys' from *The New Russian Poets 1953–1968* edited and translated by George Reavey; to Calder & Boyars, London, and October House Inc., New York. Copyright © 1966, 1968 by George Reavey.

For JOHN ALLCOCK: 'Looking Up' and 'Death is a Door'; to the Author.

For SAMUEL ALLEN (Paul Vesey): 'To Satch' from *American Gothic*; to the Author.

For W. H. AUDEN: 'The Unknown Citizen' from *Collected Shorter Poems 1927–1957*; to Faber & Faber Ltd., London, and Random House Inc., New York. Copyright 1940 and renewed 1968 by W. H. Auden.

For GASTON BART-WILLIAMS: 'god bless U S' from *New Voices of the Commonwealth*; Evans Brothers, London.

For ANDREW BASTER: 'Judas' from *Sprouts on Helicon* to Andre Deutsch Ltd., London.

For HILAIRE BELLOC: 'Is there any reward?' from *Sonnets and Verse*; to A. D. Peters & Co., London.

For JOHN BENNETT: 'he killed many of my men' from *Ulula*, the Magazine of The Grammar School, Manchester; to the Author.

For JOHN BIRKBY: 'Let's All Meet and Have a Party Sometime' from *Ulula*, the Magazine of The Grammar School, Manchester; to the Author.

For PETER BLACK: 'The Man in the Bowler Hat' from *Poetry of the Forties*; to Penguin Books Ltd.

For WILLIAM BOX: 'She Vowed Him This'; to Chester and Lang.

For EDWIN BROCK: 'To My Wife: Sonnet 3'; to The Scorpion Press, Suffolk.

For RUPERT BROOKE: 'The Voice' and 'Sonnet' from *The Collected Poems of Rupert Brooke*; to Sidgwick and Jackson Ltd., London, McLelland & Stewart Ltd., Toronto, and Dodd, Mead & Co. Inc., New York, copyright 1915 by Dodd, Mead & Co. Inc. Copyright renewed 1943 by Edward Marsh.

For GWENDOLYN BROOKS: 'We Real Cool' from *Selected Poems* to Harper & Row, Publishers, Inc., New York, copyright © 1959 by Gwendolyn Brooks.

For ALAN BROWNJOHN: 'Farmer's Point of View' from *The Lions' Mouths*; to Macmillan & Co. Ltd., London.

For CHARLES CAUSLEY: 'Hawthorn White' and 'I am the Great Sun' from *Union Street*; to David Higham Associates Ltd., London.

For TONY CONNOR: 'A Child Half-Asleep' from *Kon in Springtime*; to Oxford University Press, London.

For GREGORY CORSO: 'Second Night in N.Y.C. after 3 Years' from *Long Live Man*; to Laurence Pollinger Ltd., London, and New Directions Publishing Corporation, New York. Copyright © by New Directions Publishing Corporation.

For e e cummings: 'maggie and milly and molly and may' from *Selected Poems*; to MacGibbon & Kee, London; from *95 Poems*; to Harcourt Brace Jovanovich Inc., New York. Copyright © 1958 by e e cummings.

For P. D. CUMMINS: 'Wait' from *Some Phases of Love*; to Macmillan & Co. Ltd., London.

For ALAN DUGAN: 'Love Song, I and Thou' from *Poems*; to the Author and Yale University Press, U.S.A.

For T. S. ELIOT: 'La Figlia che Piange' and 'A Song for Simeon' from *Collected Poems 1909–1962*, copyright 1936 by Harcourt, Brace & World, Inc.; copyright © 1963, 1964 by T. S. Eliot; to Faber & Faber Ltd., London, and Harcourt Brace Jovanovich Inc., New York.

For ROSS FALCONER: 'It is impossible' from *Once Around the Sun* edited by Brian Thompson; to Brian Thompson and Oxford University Press, Australia.

For JOAN FINNIGAN: 'Noon Hour' from *New Voices of the Commonwealth*; to the Author.

For ROBERT FROST: 'Out, Out—' from *The Complete Poems of Robert Frost*; to Laurence Pollinger Ltd., London, and Holt, Rinehart & Winston Inc., New York. Copyright 1916 by Holt, Rinehart & Winston, Inc. Copyright 1944 by Robert Frost.

For ROLAND GANT: 'The Wedding'; to the Author.

For ALAN GARNER: 'Summer Solstice' and 'Rip.'; to the Author.

For ROBERT GRAVES: 'Not to Sleep' from *Man Does, Woman Is*; 'The

For KATHLEEN RAINE: 'The End of Love' from *Collected Poems 1956*; to Hamish Hamilton Ltd., London, and the Author.

For FLAVIEN RANAIVO: 'Song of a Common Lover'; to the Author.

For PETER REDGROVE: 'Bedtime Story for my Son' from *The Collector and Other Poems*; to Routledge & Kegan Paul Ltd., London.

For ELIZABETH RIDDELL: 'The Letter' from *Forebears*; to Angus & Robertson Ltd., Australia.

For ANNE RIDLER: 'For A Child Expected' from *The Nine Bright Shiners*; to Faber & Faber Ltd., London, and The Macmillan Company, New York, copyright 1941, 1961 by Anne Ridler.

For THEODORE ROETHKE: 'Child On Top of a Greenhouse' from *The Collected Poems of Theodore Roethke*; to Faber & Faber Ltd., London, and Doubleday and Co. Inc., New York, copyright 1947 by Editorial Publications Inc.

For COLIN ROWBOTHAM: 'Relative Sadness' from *Ulula*, the Magazine of The Grammar School, Manchester; to the Author.

For TADEUSZ ROZEWICZ: 'Leave Us Alone' from *Postwar Polish Poetry*, translated by Czeslaw Milosz; Penguin Books 1970 and Doubleday & Co. Inc., New York, 1965; to the Translator.

For CLIVE SANSOM: 'The Font' from *The Cathedral*; to David Higham Associates Ltd., London.

For SIEGFRIED SASSOON: 'The Effect' from *Collected Poems of Siegfried Sassoon 1908–1956*; to Faber & Faber Ltd., London, and the Viking Press Inc., New York. Copyright 1918 by E. P. Dutton & Co., renewed 1946 by Siegfried Sassoon.

For LÉOPOLD SÉDAR-SENGHOR: 'Totem' from *Modern Poetry from Africa*, edited and translated by Gerald Moore and Ulli Beier; to the Author and Penguin Books, and to Editions du Seuil, Paris.

For GEORGE SEFERIS: 'Mythistorema' from *Poems*, translated by Rex Warner; to The Bodley Head Ltd., London, and Little Brown & Co., Boston. English translation © Rex Warner 1960.

For PRADIP SEN: 'The Man on My Back'; to the Author.

For JACK SIMCOCK: 'To My Wife' and 'Still Branches'; to the Author.

For STEVIE SMITH: 'Not Waving But Drowning' and 'The Jungle Husband' from *Selected Poems*; to Longmans Green & Co. Ltd., London, and New Directions Publishing Corporation, New York. © 1962, 1964 by Stevie Smith.

For WOLE SOYINKA: 'Koko Oloro' from *Idanre and Other Poems*; to Methuen & Co. Ltd., London, and Hill & Wang Inc., New York. © Wole Soyinka 1967.

For SU TUNG-P'O: 'On the Birth of His Son' from *170 Chinese Poems*, translated by Arthur Waley; to Constable Publishers, London, and

Index of Poets and Titles

197

Index of First Lines